CW00382340

Voices from the dolls' house

Also by Adèle Geras

The Egerton Hall Trilogy:
The Tower Room
Watching the Roses
Pictures of the Night

The Fantora Family Files
Fantora Family Photographs

My Grandmother's Stories

The Christmas Cat
Voyage

Toey

Little Elephant's Moon
Fishpie for Flamingoes
The Strange Bird
The Glittering River

A Magic Birthday

Yesterday (a memoir)

Adèle Geras

Voices from the dolls' house

For Linda,

love from

Adèle Geras.

Rockingham Press

Published in 1994
by
The Rockingham Press
11 Musley Lane,
Ware, Herts
SG12 7EN

British Library Cataloguing-in-Publication Data

A catalogue record for this book
is available from the British Library

ISBN 1 873468 26 1

Printed in Great Britain
by Bemrose Shafron (Printers) Ltd,
Chester

Printed on Recycled Paper

This book is dedicated
to the memory of my father,
Laurence Weston
(1910-1972)

Acknowledgements

Some of these poems have appeared in the following magazines: *Ambit, Spokes, Orbis, The Literary Review, Numbers, The North, Other Poetry, Vision On, Writing Women, The Rialto, Staple, Signal, Lancaster Litfest anthologies, Arvon Poetry Competition 1987 Runners-up Anthology.*

'Needleworks' has appeared in 'Northern Poetry One' eds. Catherine Byron and John Lyons (Littlewood 1989) and in 'New Women Poets' ed. Carol Rumens (Bloodaxe 1990)

'Four Voices' has appeared in 'Give me Shelter' ed. Michael Rosen (Bodley Head 1991)

'Voices from the Dolls' House' has appeared in 'Northern Poetry Two' eds. Debjani Chatterjee and William Scammell (Littlewood 1991)

Several of the poems have appeared in two pamphlets: 'Up on the Roof' (joint winner with Pauline Stainer of Smith/Doorstop Poetry Pamphlet Competition, 1987) 'Sampler' (Priapus Press 1991)

'Hannah Smith's Sampler' won second prize in the Orbis Rhyme Revival competition 1992

'Egyptian Cat' and 'Elegy for Miss Ratcliffe' won first prizes in Literary Review monthly poetry competitions, and together with 'Kindertransport', appear in The Literary Review Anthology of Real Poetry (1990)

'Photograph 1900' won third prize in Ver Open competition 1992

'From a shop in Jerusalem' won the Jewish Quarterly H.H. Wingate Poetry Prize (1993)

Contents

Patchwork

She starts with red.
Everything begins with strange mixtures of blood:
vein branches under white skin, white sheets spotted scarlet,
a rose opening slowly on a green ground,
flowering over the fabric.

She takes blue for skies,
small squares of daylight in a sloping wall,
long washes of midnight ocean broken by anxious moons turning.
Blue firmaments, pale blue for the sorrow,
lapis lazuli of ancient denim.

Sometimes yellow chooses her.
Lunatic daisies grin in white bonnets,
and saffron, ochre, persimmon blaze under her scorched hands.
Soothe them with butter, comfortable primrose.
Avoid the sun. Seek shadows.

Is she superstitious about green?
She drowns in colours of water. Debatable shades: turquoise,
peacock, teal, aquamarine. Shuns emerald, lime and olive.
Sometimes grass green is a background.
She tries to look away.

She needs black everywhere:
a fence around flowers, barrier between one colour
and another. A thin reminder that through azure and crimson
our days are stitched with black and we have black
as a lining for our closed eyes.

Lacemaker, Bruges, 1986

She understands
the placing of the pins, and can foresee
flowers and small boats
windmills and butterflies
in the thin twisting,
in the clicking of the bobbin-clusters
moved round,
and back again.

The nuns taught her
in the days when barbed wire
frequently displayed
the patterns made by flesh,
and blood arranged itself
in crimson webs and meshes
on the skin.

Her threads cross
where they are meant to cross.
Gold pins
prick out the spaces
between white and white.
Veins on her hands
swell into blue lace.

We are silent
watching her.

An elegy for Miss Ratcliffe

You are the perfect ghost and understand
the quiet rituals of your return.
You sit with me sometimes, and in the dusk,
opals burn cloudy fires on your hand.

You were at home in rooms designed for tea:
translucent china, fields of Axminster.
I made up lovers for you in my head,
killed in the War, poor things, or lost at sea.

You spoke of Laocöon: I saw it all —
the limbs contorted on the beach at Troy
were visible just where the blackboard was,
and serpent's scales silvered the classroom wall.

Drawing the curtains closed, I feel your shade
approving birds and sprays of peonies.
Your hand is on your hair, patting the bun,
checking the complications of the braid.

Kindertransport

Josef loves trains. He cannot wait to leave.
He asks about the sea. "Will it be blue?
Is England far? Who will look after us?
And why is it that Mama can't come too?"

My mother says the steam is in her eyes
and that is why she cannot help the tears.
"Look after Josef. Be polite and good."
The words crack open, shatter in my ears.

"How long" asks Josef "will the journey last?"
I should have used my eyes with greater care,
remembered all the small things from my life.
My mother's fading, shrinking..."soon be there.."

Mother N

She shakes out
muesli dunes from cardboard boxes.
Jars on her shelves
hold the ingredients of landscape.

She makes seashores
pebbled with pulses: haricots and yellow lentils
kidney beans dark as blood, and black eyed peas
drift to shingle in her bowls.

She has cut down cauliflower branches
milky as jade, covered them
with the slip and shine of sauce,
and small volcanic outcrops in the dish
are rimmed with the beginnings of brown crusts.

Emerald stems of broccoli
gather into forests.

Each morning,
she peels a grapefruit sun,
and lamps of oranges light her kitchen.

At night,
her daughter eats apple crescents
arranged round the circumference of a plate
like overlapping slices of the moon.

Years ago

street lights crossed the wing mirror
in dotted lines, repetitive as memories.

You'd wake from your child sleep
just to see the orange stripes
approach, then slide away behind the car.

You'd stand on the back seat
looking at where we'd come from
with both hands pressed against the glass:
small flowers open in the dark.

Composer

She is chopping onions, listening to Mozart's 'Requiem'.
She imagines the kitchen ceiling vaulted and gilded,
ornately scrolled, thronged with angels.

Her knitted shawl on the table,
(magenta, turquoise, silver, blue and black, randomly striped)
is nothing but a soft place for her sleeping cat
who knows everything about harmony,
and can recognize a pleasing contrast
with her own dark tiger-markings
when she sees one.

Moving the sofa

She has moved the sofa
to face south.

Yesterday, summer was there,
over her right shoulder,
out of the corner of her eye,
beyond the cacti and the succulents.

Today, she looks at it
directly:
laburnum, lilac, and behind their leaves,
(spread like a fan to hide the fact
that they are past their best)
the last camellias.

In her high windows,
stained green and amethyst and blue and rose,
she watches flowers offering
the consolation of glass.

Needleworks

Hannah Smith's Casket 1657

'The yere of Our Lord being 1657
if ever I have any thoughts about the time
when I went to Oxford, as it may be I may,
when I have forgotten the time,
to satisfi my self, I may look in this paper
and find it.
I went to Oxford in the yere of 1644 ...

The King and his court are here.
My cousin Beth lives
in a house beside the walls.
My mother left me.
Father says
she looks on me from Heaven.

I keep her box of silks,
pages of printed patterns
like a book.

Here is Winter,
an old man in a bonnet
rocking in a chair.
At his feet, a brazier,
at his back, a river
waiting for the colour of ice.
I shall sew red
into the fire
and flames like a fountain
will edge his robes with saffron.

Winter has a cat.
It sits and watches him,
watches empty trees,
tall houses, a bellows
waiting for embers
and logs bound into bundles.

Satin	satin stitch
embroidery silk	stem stitch
metal threads	laid work
seed pearls	padding
spangles	petit point

The lions' heads
are threaded with bronze.
Birds fly in the border,
pearls in white wings.

Lady Autumn's
finely attired
among her golden sheaves.
Behind her,
blue silk
and green silk
of the river.
Trees branch to feathers,
clouds like veils
touch a pink castle.
Always evening light
for Lady Autumn.

and my being there 2 yeres,
for I went in 1644
and I stayed there 1645
and cam away in 1646,
and I was almost 12 yeres of age when I went
and made an end of my cabinette at Oxford ...

Stitches
tell stories:

Joseph and his brothers
at the well,
Deborah and Barak,
and Jael and Sisera.

The tent flutters,
open. *He asked
for water and she gave him milk
and butter in a lordly dish*
then killed him.

Cousin Beth
is caring for a soldier
wounded in battle.
I help her.
I keep the watches
beside his bed
and mark his fevered breathing.

Sometimes I think:
his life is my silk,
tied to my needle.
Stitches gather.
I make the pictures
to fill the hours
till my life shall start:
when the war ends,
when the soldier wakes,
when he looks on me.

*and my cabinette was mad up in the yere of 1656
at London.*

The soldier left our house.
I embroidered long weeks:
every thread a vein
every pearl a tear
every stitch a sorrow
every needle a small dagger
drawing blood.

My cabinet holds trinkets:
letters, chains,
locks of hair, and flowers
pressed to memories.

I have ritten this to satisfi my self
and those that shall inquir about it.

Hannah Smith

Sampler 1850

If I look up
from the window seat, I see the garden.
The flowers are ragged after rain.
Soon, autumn will be here.
Already, leaves have fallen on the path.

I turn to my sampler.
The flowers are in lines
evenly spaced, and when I've finished them
I'll write my name, and numbers
and the date.
When winter comes, I will have started
my picture of a house.

Where shall I go
when I reach the edge of the canvas?

Wallhanging 1920

A story told and told:

My great-grandmother, always called The Bobbeh,
demonstrates devotion,
attention to detail
and a sense of smell that was the envy of Jerusalem.

She was blind in old age.
Her daughter held and twisted
the domestic threads.

At nighttime, beds like waterlilies
opened in the dining-room.
Tight-folded sheets unfurled in corridors.
Unerringly, The Bobbeh
crossed yellow tiles and reached the linen chest.

There she would sniff each pillow and pronounce
every child's name in turn, with no mistakes.
'This one is Sara's' (recognizing smells)
'Reuben's and Dina's' ... on and on
a murmuring variation on ten notes.

Outside the story:
the white filigree of crochet,
the squares and diamonds of drawn-threadwork
bordering each pillowslip
on every perfectly distributed pillow

have stiffened now, smell of green soap
and the grey weight of the iron,
pressing flat. The work of her young hands.

Her seeing shrank. Her needle swelled
thick as a chicken bone.

It plunged through canvas dragging blanket wool,
made crosses in child's colours:
the peaks and dips of hastily-drawn hills.

The Bobbeh's cross-stitch mountains
covered a whole wall
in the end.
Uneven green and red, orange and black,
purple, white and yellow chevrons
rose from the horizon of her couch
almost to the ceiling.

Tapestry 1971

She had intended it for me
because she had no children of her own.
'Take it with you,' she said
'I don't need it.' If I die (she meant)
someone else will have the trouble
of packing, of dispatching.
And what if it were lost?
Or the glass could break,
some unforeseen sharp thing
tear the canvas ... oh,
the whole tapestry could reach you
shredded.

She prepares for dreamed cataclysms.
Now, I'm here.
Tomorrow, I'm going home,
so let me take it.

They check it at the airport.
Are there terrorists

who parcel bombs
like pictures, framed?
Arrange explosives flat
behind the glass?
The men on duty
unwrap it, wrap it up again
unlovingly.
Patterns elude them,
colours slide past their eyes,
It is not what they feared.

It hangs in an alcove.
The jade tree on the TV set
almost reaches it.

'Petit point' she said,
giving it to me.
The stitches are smaller than sesame seeds:
huddled apostrophes, slanting to the right.
The canvas was starched gauze —
a fine white mesh.
'I don't lilke printed patterns..being told
where to go and in what shade of pink.
I follow from one colour to the next.
When one thread ends
another calls to me.
I never know, never knew
the path the silk would take,
how it would come out.
Mother said I'd tire of it.
She died too soon to see it on the wall.
Towards the end,
criss-crossing lines appeared
in black: a colour
I'd been trying to avoid.'

I think:
there was a plan known
by the fingers. The little glitter
of a needle's eye
foresaw circles
triangles
dots
moons
balconies
stars
curves
rectangles
upended squares
sloping to rows of geometric hills.

Look: this yellow disc
could be a lamp
or an apricot
or the sun.

Embroidered picture 1987

You and I see houses
in a suburban street:
privet hedges, nineteen-thirties windows,
trees taken for granted,
Sunday-painted gates,
blue thrown over everything
like a scarf: unremarked.

She saw
curves, lines, perspectives,
twenty possibilities of green,
pink roofs shrinking to distance,
threads massing into branches.
She framed everything with lace —
a thin cloud border for the pale washed sky.

Oscar Wilde speaks from Père Lachaise Cemetery

I feel that if one has to be a ghost
It's best to drift around delightful stones.
I count myself more fortunate than most
That Death in Paris has arranged my bones.

The company is just what one expects:
Colette, Chopin, Seurat and lovely Jim
Who died so young. Now Youth pays its respects
In multitudes who still remember him.

I like the well-planned look of every street:
Beneath the trees, long terraces of tombs.
I whisper wittily to those I meet
Lying unvisited in marble rooms.

But I'd give all this up (you'll think me silly)
For half an hour's walk down Piccadilly.

A letter from Helen of Troy

Menelaus, darling
I do think this is all a bit excessive!
I can see you from the walls, you know,
don't think I can't,
besieging away like mad, down on the plain.
Ye Gods, I thought, watch out, the gang's all here:
Hector and Agamemnon and Achilles
and that young man of his whose name escapes me,
the old bore, Nestor, even Ulysses.
I know why he's around. It's her, of course.
Penelope. Bloody needlework all day long.
He needs an outlet for his energy.
I do sympathise,
but still...

I've heard the gossip.
Yes, even up here in good old Topless Towers
it reaches us,
don't think it doesn't.
That dreadful business with Iphigenia.
Well, wind you asked for then
and wind you've got
and serve you right
and all for what?

I fancied Paris.
I would have got over it.
I've fancied other men before.
(You know that. I don't have to tell you.)
I think it was his thighs
like well-turned wood ...
but there you go ...
you cannot build
relationships on rippling flesh.
I've learned.
I'd have come back.

But you've overreacted as usual.
Now it's busy, busy, busy
hammering wood together all day long.
And what with that
and Cassandra moaning
and Hecuba criticising
and Priam losing his memory
and Paris going off me
on account of the fighting,
I'm bored to tears.

The rumour said a thousand ships.
I think war turns you on, Menelaus,
you and all the men.

It isn't about me at all.
Is it?

A corner of the artist's room in Paris

(Gwen John)

She has designed
(she who thought herself a shadow)
a setting suitable
for the writing of love letters
to an unsuitable lover.
Lace whispers down the window.
A faintly-patterned light falls
in faint patterns on the yellow table.

> He is a maker
> of soft flesh from stone.
> He finds warm places with a chisel,
> breaks into alabaster veins
> looking for feelings.

She has arranged
around the wicker chair where she will sit
a parasol
a shawl
a vase of flowers:
props appropriate
for delicate thoughts
and baisers du printemps.

> His hands
> have picked her up and stroked her briefly
> (small, speckled pebble lost among marble slabs)
> and left her in a corner of his mind.
> Of course, he thinks of her from time to time

She has imagined
hands on her skin like doves.
He will be back, a giant
shaking the yellow silence of her room.
When all the light has gone, he'll take the shawl
and spread it over her before he leaves.

Tea with Henry Moore

At first,
she sits upright on the chair.
Lamplight shows in the space around her heart.

Scone crags,
pastel symmetries of Battenburg
rise on white porcelain plains.

She looks
into the luminous hollow of a cup.
Her face
curves and stretches over a silver spoon.

After tea,
she is recumbent, and the marble dusk
bruises the slope of hip and thigh —

oh, the enormous sliding-down of mountains!

The Thirteenth

It's years since I saw the place
and even so, not long enough for me.
What a bore he is, my brother, with his roses!
A flower doomed to disappoint,
whose petals pucker, shrivel, fall
and bleed their colours into earth.
Thorns are reliable,
curving and blackening to daggers
one should take into account.

My sisters, and the sisters
on the other side of the family
will roll through the corridors
with dizzyingly predictable parcels.
They'll have bought new dresses,
lilac, pink, and blue. Kidding themselves
they look good for their age: not quite buds
but roses in the days before collapse —
Madame Plantier, or Duchesse d'Angoulême.

They're not expecting me.
They must have said: "Don't tell her.
She sits in Paris, never visits us..
don't tell her. How will she find out?"
But I can smell new rosebuds on the wind.
Oh, I can see them, hear them: "Black
for a christening! Whatever next?"
My gift will spread white silence like a shroud.
Death — always a splendid conversation-stopper.

Fantasy

(for Madge Gill, artist, 1884 -1961)

Eyelids are apples
sliced to moon crescents.
Pips fall
on cold floors
and won't be flowers,
not ever.

Lines start in the corner,
coaxed from the black dot
into threads like rain
stretched out on windows.

The pen trails
ferns and fronds and fringes,
lace and lattices and nets of diamond,
feathers and fans and steps that grow and shrink
and staircases like snail shells spiralling
across the calico
unwinding and unwinding and unwinding.

Faces in a filigree of ink
have eyes, and all the eyes
and all the eyes are open.

Hannah Smith's sampler, 1810

(This is a real sampler, in the Victoria and Albert Museum, and the sestina uses the motto stitched into the sampler as a 'tornada'.)

Where the long darkness and the lamplight meet
the line is drawn, a circle round my world,
and in this world, everything I attempt
demands an order and should be appropriately sweet.
I am told to think good thoughts, as I sit here
and from the silks gathered in my basket, pluck

one thread. When I lean forward to pluck
the favoured strand, the colours stir, and where they meet
and twist, I find the small ends of rainbows here
among unravelling skeins. In the canvas world,
I shall start with a house, a garden sweet
with flowers. Later, I must attempt

figures of Adam and Eve. I shall attempt
the Tree of Knowledge, and the apple, ready to pluck
sending the scarlet promise of a taste sweet
in the mouth, from where two branches meet
and leaves shake out a greenness on the world.
Above my Paradise, I will embroider here

a vase in terra cotta red, and over here
a marble urn in shades of white and grey. To attempt
curves is foolish, in and out of little squares of a world
where needles travel in diagonals. I pluck
another silk from the basket, a pink to meet
the requirements of a rose embodying all things sweet.

Tapestry birds are blue and sing more sweet
for being silken, for being always here.
I will sew my name at the centre. Borders will meet

gently at the corners. Look at the butterflies! I'll not attempt
to catch them. As for the rose, there's none can pluck
the frilled head from the stem. A world

surrounds a stitched rose quite unlike the world
that is mine. All is pressed flat. What is sweet
remains so. Thorns are not sharp, and to pluck
them, and to prick your fingers is impossible here.
I have fashioned a geometric alphabet, an attempt
to pick out a motto both melodious and meet:

'What is the world, or all things here?
'Tis but a bitter sweet. When I attempt
a rose to pluck, a pricking thorn I meet.'

White stone

Heptonstall, September 20th

She found a white stone,
a suitable small moon
and kept it ready.

She said the names aloud,
a register of women
lying in their last beds:

Maud, Frances, May, Dora, Ellen, Rose,
Violet Gertrude, Emily, Emily, Emily,
Mary, Annie, Anne, beloved wife,

treasured memories and also Elizabeth
his beloved daughter, also Elizabeth,
and pray for the soul of Edith,

and Eliza rest in peace, and Sarah,
also Elizabeth, Florence, Hannah and Marie,
rest in peace, beloved wife, fond memories.

Names whisper in the long grass,
muffled by heather erupting from the graves.
Mary Ann. Beloved. Beloved something.

In the end, she found the only Sylvia
and set the stone under the yellow rose
still flaunting pale flames, still brave.

Torn rags of cloud dusted across the sun.
The world turned, sliding down from summer
towards the equinox.

Four voices

If that one gives me owt, I'll show my arse
in M and S's window.

*

I don't know what   a disgrace
I call it   the world's coming to
some of these kids   look at the starving
Africans   got a cheek don't know
they're born   look at the Kurds
I don't know   before the War
not to mention   poor dumb animals
absolutely shocking   where
do they all come from?

*

I can read her mind, see?
like her thoughts were them balloons
you get sometimes, puffy pink and silver.

*

Bye baby bunting
Daddy's buggered off.

Rock a bye baby
only quietly.
Walls are thin.

Rub a dub dub
forty people
use this bath.

Hickory dickory dock
the mouse ran

behind the skirting-board
when I opened the door.

Baa baa black sheep
bloody typical of you
said my Mum.
No one else in this
family ever
got in trouble.

*

id know a house
if i saw one   once
i was in a home
im a snail now
with a sleeping bag
curled up on my back
finding spaces
out of the rain
one pound fifty ninell
buy a burger an chips but
the needle cant wait what
did it feel like
to be really full

*

There's him outside Humana
with a dead cute dog
that just sits there
looking hungry. My old cat
would never stand for it.
She'd walk off if she wanted.
She's the one I think of.
She's the one I miss.

She's not the one I'm leaving.
She never hurt me.

*

Haven't they got   whatever do they
smell like   homes to go to?

*

Bed and breakfast baby
better beware.
One little squeak
and they'll take you into care.

One little smack
on your pink little bum
then
in comes the doctor
in comes the nurse
and the magistrate lady
with the alligator purse
to take you away
from your poor old Mum.

So hush pretty baby
don't dare to cry.
I'll have towels like that
sheets like that
shoes like that
look at all the windows, lovey.
See that bed there? In't it smashing?
We'll have that one, thank you kindly
in the sweet bye and bye.

*

I'd write to my mum if I had a stamp.
Dear Mum, I'd say, do you know that your house
your red brick terrace, all neat and prim,
(two up, two down,
privet hedges, garden path,

blue hydrangea by the door,
ding-dong silly
doorbell chimes,
microwave oven,
colour telly,
fluffy covers
on the loo-seat, and all that)
is a monster's cave where the walls run blood?

*

see him over there
with his crimplene trousers
baggy an hanging
off his arse
he'd do it with anything
must be good for a bob or two
o jesus i hope
i hope he is

*

Mum, do you know
about slimy fingers,
smelly breath, scaly skin?
Do you recognise him you married?
Him in the photo, slick and smug,
my Dad? I'm not stopping in his cave.

My squat's a bloody paradise
compared. I've got mates.
On a good day,
I have chips and a cuppa
and an apple off the barrows.
I can slice money
thin as bacon.
I can spot a decent fag-end
at a hundred paces.

I can smile nicely,
make rich mothers think:
that could be my daughter.
Then I'm laughing.

*

And in my day   no better than
they should   you kept yourself
to yourself   clean some of this lot.
It's drugs   and it's
the system   and it's
the lack of discipline and it's
not enough love   and it's
what the world is coming to
I don't know   and it's

*

after the needle
im ok im better
needle shines in my eyes
like a candle
i get a fiver if im lucky
an the back seat of a car
else its bum against the bricks
ta very much and heres
a bit of change

needles need
thats why theyre called that
need feeding dont they
like fucking slot machines
like juke boxes
put a penny in an
up goes my skirt
an here comes the music
listen o

i fancy a needle
something rotten give us one

*

I blame the parents and
I blame the teachers and
I blame the Government and
I blame television and
I blame   I blame and
why don't they all get jobs?
There.
That's the answer. Fancy
no one thinking of that before!
When it comes right   at the end of
down to it the day
I blame the Council.
They clear the litter, don't they?

*

Baby, I wish you
a front door
you can lock.

A gas fire
and matches.

I wish you a fridge
with milk in it.

A biscuit tin
full of Kitkats.

Pretty green cartons
full of orange juice.

Enough money
at the checkout

so you never have
to put anything back.

Oh, my little darling
I wish you
your own room
with a Care Bear
on the pillow.

Sweet baby
please don't cry.

The window

Every other heartbeat,
the baby breathes
veils over glass.
Someone, somewhere else,
sowed flower borders
on her cotton bonnet:
silk cross-stitches
like gold
and like carnations.
Like the sky.

From this window
the mother sees
blurred streets.
The room behind her
flattens to dark:
backdrop for a headscarf
pleated and ridged in white
like bone,
like folded paper,
like the loss.

In the queue for water

Sarajevo, December 1992

They come with blistered saucepans.
They come with kerosene tins.
Nobody has a plastic bucket
as new and blue and fine as mine.

Oh, my grandmother's samovar,
my mother's wine glasses,
my American Pyrex!

The soles of their shoes are like paper.
Their stockings are lumpy with darns.
Nobody here has leather brogues
as polished and brown and fine as mine.

Oh, my grandfather's riding-boots,
my father's Oxfords,
my Italian shoes!

Most jackets have lost their buttons.
Collars and cuffs are frayed.
Nobody has a full-length coat
as dark and woollen and fine as mine.

Oh, my grandmother's crochet shawls,
my mother's tweed ensembles,
my British raincoat!

Watches have vanished for flour,
necklaces melted to grease.
Nobody has a bracelet of gold
as heavy and twisted and fine as mine.

Oh, my grandmother's rubies,
my mother's wedding ring,
my Swiss diamonds!

Scarves are as thin as bandages.
Colours are scrubbed away.
Nobody has a white fox fur
as cunning and warm and fine as mine.

Oh, my grandmother's Persian lamb,
my mother's ermine stole,
my Russian mink!

*

I am thinking: perhaps I was conceived
the night before the Archduke's carriage
brought him to this town.

Old Basmannaya Street: Olga, packing to leave

We are folding everything most carefully
and the ghosts, dust-mouthing:
"Us, take us with you."
Especially her clothes, which I will wear one day.
Sleeves break from silk waves into crusts of lace
and I hide them, bend them out of sight.
"Put us in gently, and try
not to crush us."
Mamushka, your arms
are in pleats behind your back!
Petticoat waterfalls, scarf mists, and lakes
of satin skirts, abracadabra
vanish in the valise. And the ghosts:
"Cover us up. Don't let us out. Not yet."

Black ribbons fly on the ceiling
marking the places where the lamps were lit.
The ghosts are breathing: "Take us off the wall,
out of the drawers.
Roll us up with the carpet.
We will come out flat,
like pressed flowers."

The furniture is waiting at the station
in the shroud-silence of straw.

We will unbury everything
later.

The ghosts will blow veils on the mirrors:
"Please (whispering) please see us.
Fold us carefully
into the creases of your lives.
Take us with you."

Natalya dressing

The Old Man brings a spade to every picnic,
dreams of unfamiliar cacti.

I have followed him everywhere,
nowhere taken root.

In my country
streets were ribbons of steel
and sharp black trees rose in the fields.
Here, the hibiscus burns. Bougainvillea
spills over balconies like blood.
Skies are turquoise at daybreak,
indigo at dusk. Shadows fly
from the white sun.

I shall wear my dark skirt
and a jacket that closes like armour
over a pale silk blouse.
Trimmings of lace lie thin
as mist on water.
My brooch will leave two pinpricks in the fabric
but it can't be helped.
I need the collar
tight around my neck.
This hat reminds me
of European boulevards and yellow lamplight,
and waltzes played on bandstands in the park.

Pull the veil down.
Only this fine black mesh
can hold my face in its accustomed shape.

I am a wax doll.
Pain is a candle
held too near my eyes
and I am melting in the heat.
Melting.

Cleaning the rice Jerusalem, 1948

She is old enough to clean the rice.
They have poured it over her shoulder
on to the round tray,
and it rattled on the brass
like small-arms fire, coming from far away.

There are patterns scratched into the metal
of interlocking snakes and leaves
and loops that start here, and end
nowhere, curving into where they came from.

She pushes paths through the grains,
making golden passageways
with low,white walls.
With the flat of both hands
she levels hills of tiny pearls
into a blanket, snow on fire,
and picks out blackened grains
and stunted ones,
and places them outside the blazing rim
that guards their perfect brothers.

Then she picks up two handfuls,
holds them high
and lets the hard rain fall
on interlocking snakes and leaves and loops,
with a noise like small-arms fire,
heard as you turn
between sleep and sleep.

9, Chancellor Street, Jerusalem: Up on the Roof

We've hidden broken clothespegs
under a bucket. They smell of old soap,
they are bleached dry, like small bones,
good for throwing down into the street.
Listen for the tiny sound they make
below us.
Sometimes a man wearing a hat goes by.
(A black felt crown and a brown fur brim:
a creature curled around his head.)
There's twenty points if a clothespeg
settles in the fur,
and ten if we can make him look
to see what God is up to.
Down there is the garden
where the rabbits are, and the smell
like yesterday's smoke,
of pine needles and sand.

We can see the corner
of the pavement by the hospital.
They bring sick people wrapped in stiffened sheets
to sit outside, to yellow in the sun.
They prop them up against the golden walls,
so we cross over to the other side.
We don't like looking.

We know exactly who
goes into Genzel's shop, but it's too far
to see the things they buy.

The city is embroidered on the sky
and when we go downstairs
someone will roll it up

put it in a basket
and only take it out again
when we come back.

From a shop in Jerusalem

My sister has turned her back to the door.
Avoid it, she says, the street is full of History
walking up and down. Some of it
will come in. She has made
a barricade in the window, riveted
lace with brooch-pins, stuck cushions
full of earrings, heaped hillocks
of ancient underwear against the glass,
scattered painted dolls in the folds
of tablecloths fretted with drawn threadwork.
The window swells with the weight of fabric.
Between the glass and everything,
an orange plastic sheet keeps out the sun.

Do you want it all to fade?
my sister says.

Shlomzion the Queen is in the Bible.
The street called after her slopes
into the noise of the city.
Heat slaps the window, climbs the golden stones,
blows through the spaces between pine needles,
past the kiosk on the corner selling drinks
like dissolved rubies, fizzing in paper cups,
and over railings guarding
a scrubby square of land studded (who knows why?)
with ancient gravestones.

But not in here, my sister says.
She says: I am remembering the snow.

We came when I was four and she was six.
There has been snow from time to time
in this city, placed high, high,
to be within easy reach of God.

But snow! Snow over your ankles,
up to your knees, billowing like a quilt
shaken over everything, a freight of white
on the roofs, frost doilies on the window.
I remember them, my sister says,
pouring white stories into the melting nights,
singing of forests and wolves
in a land of sand and jackals,
milk and honey, and a sun like a flatiron,
pressing and pressing.

My sister has filled the shop
with a blizzard of linen, and children's toys
come from the Old Country: glossy
with magenta, turquoise, the yellow of Russian amber.
Fat dolls you can split in two, like cracked eggs
and take out a doll which splits in two
and on and on down to a tiny one
no bigger than a thimble.

We have other stock.
Tables with legs carved into spirals,
brass trays scratched with patterns
of interlocking stems and leaves and curves
that start here and end nowhere.
We have (somewhere) lacquer boxes,
sandalwood chests and a selection
of jewellery in all the latest styles,
my sister says.

We have been busy.
The shop is stocked to the ceiling.
If you open a box, my sister says,
and breathe in the fragrance of trees,
you can banish the smell of gas
and sweep ash into corners never looked into.

Concentrate, my sister says, on pins
and see how the bayonets vanish!

Love all the curving stomachs of the dolls.
Stroke them, see how full they are.
Our children, if we had had them,
would have come out dark with blood.
Flowers are better, my sister says.

Every so often, in the street outside
the fighting starts again.
My sister says: we live in a place
where armies drive about outside the window.
Avoid wars, she says. Stay away from the door.
Re-arrange the barricades a little.
Put in a few new nick-nacks. Oh, I love
the copper candlesticks, and camels
chiselled from stones streaked with the blue
of my imagined seas.

Shawls have come from Japan.
Embroidered flowers enormous
in slippery silk gardens, fringes
falling like soft foliage from the edges.
Everywhere else, my sister says,
bullets are blooming. Death braids crimson garlands,
sets them on cold brows, winds them round stiffened arms.

Hang the shawls
up there in the corner, my sister says.

Put the roses facing the street.

Cartographer

(for Anne Fine)

She has charted the terrain:
marked the site of Wounds,
mapped the crevasses of Despair,
pinpointed the source of Tears
falling in streams towards the gravel shores
of Irritation. Her pen
has etched the warnings:
here be the Dragons of Lust,
here be the Whirlpools of Unreason,
and here the Dark Mulligrubs —
(Traveller, beware these ancient trees
weeping leaves sharp as black knives.)

Somewhere (find it! find it!)
lies the Sea of Tenderness.
Three Winds blow in the corners.
There's Longing, trailing heliotrope skirts
over the Mountains of Misunderstanding,
Frustration, puffing useless breath
against the granite promontory of Time,
and Laughter, bright-haired, holding in her hand
the horn of Disillusion, blowing gold.

Creative Writing Class

Today, she thinks,
they will write
about picnics
and if their windows open
on to walls, on to concrete,
I have pictures in my folder.

The sky today is sugary with heat
and the sun a slice of lemon, crystallized.

Pretend, she says,
the classroom walls have melted
and waves of grass swell
between your desk and the horizon,
and there are trees for shade.

I have pictures in my folder. Look.

Who, she says,
are the girls with flesh like apricots
and skirts like smoke?

What, she says,
does the watermelon look like?
A big, red smile, do you think?
Or flesh?
Use your own words.

But, she says,
if you'd rather
describe a picnic you've been on yourself
there's nothing wrong with that.

Real life, she says,
is harder.
But try it if you like.

Sonnet

Hold both my hands. Be careful of the pins.
My mother's making candles from my nails.
She's blocked the outside drain with wedding veils.
I smile at all the crooning wheelie bins;
I'm filleting silk fish with amber fins.
My twenty ships, rigged with macramé sails,
are taking tests which every zebra fails
and winning oranges from metal twins.

Tomorrow, I will make a loaf of bread
from coloured glass and smoke and PVC
and five dead flowers and my income tax.

I'll let you have the passkey to my head.
Watch out for flowerpots that look like me.
Stick shrieking bubble gum in all the cracks.

Wings

I hardly ever take them out these days.
They're in the hall cupboard
next to the wellingtons and walking-sticks.
The feathers have yellowed:
petals fallen from white roses.

I intend to buy a black pair very soon,
with a sheen on them like oil slicks.
I shall wear them constantly;
also a matching necklace in Victorian jet.

The Green Party

allow velvet curtains
to gather at the windows
like moss

unroll oceans
of taffeta to cover
your body drift
chiffon like seaweed
from your hair

fill vases
with ferns
dark ivy
polished evergreens

serve olives
in painted dishes
asparagus broccoli
spinach cauliflower
a salad of emeralds
malachite and jade

then green figs
gooseberry fool
and apples

on your way
to the garden
consider the aquarium
green glass water
hung with silver fish

drink crème de menthe
under the trees
walk among herbs
crush tarragon
remember rosemary

after the party
hang your dress
over a chair
the skirt is a lake
of eau de nil
on the scarlet carpet

Jade

Quietly behind glass,
veins of white jade grow into branches
around the swell of a bottle.

Doll-sized,
translucent and opaque, it offers
the promise of transparency.

Tips of carved leaves
are pointed towards green.

Judge

Although I have done nothing wrong,
there is a Judge in the attic.

When I hang upside down,
dreams fall out of my head.

I'm selling my wedding dress. Size 10.
White. Magnificent. Never worn.

I have square days on white paper
under photographs of empty landscapes.

Other days are long and thin
set in a border of black leaves.

I spread dustsheets in the garden
so that the flowers won't fade.

I have an umbrella for every occasion
and gloves for letter-writing,

also for chopping chili peppers,
moving my puppets, covering my hands.

The Judge in the attic waits to be unfolded
although I have done nothing wrong.

The Awaited Guest

(from a painting by Vaī Archer)

She will sit, when she arrives
on a chair with barley-sugar strands of wood
winding down the back.
A dress awaits her on a hanger
padded with red silk.
Padded, because the fabric of her dress
will crush or bruise
will spoil or stain
so easily.
The frills and folds of it
copy the curves of her body
and the colours of her flesh.

The tablecloth is white.
Diamonds within diamonds
of drawn threadwork.
The food is strawberries
and raw, white mushrooms
and prawns
lying on the plate like whiskery petals
of a tropical flower, spread out
and spiralling.

Five prawns are waiting for him
when he arrives.
His empty shirt sleeves rest on the table
waiting for him.

When he comes
if he comes,
he'll find a knife only.

There is a fork where she will sit,
old-fashioned silver
which will be heavy in the hand.

Two other places are set at the table
for someone. For guests.
There is a napkin in a silver ring.

If you weren't looking closely
if you didn't know,
you would never see
the silver slice of discontented face
reflected in the knife-blade,
lying in the foreground
right under your eyes.

My grandmother's mirror

says:

Darling child, there were days
when every leaf was gold and every garland,
and at my back a quiet lake of silver.
All the pastel girls danced for me
in lines like flowers,
to music from a piano echoing
the disappearing years. This was a room
with a high, high ceiling, darling.

My grandmother
looks into the mirror,
and sees, a long way off,
a child opening a door
on to a darkened corridor
with all the light behind her.

Care instructions for the 'Desirée' Mirror

(Adjustable/Wing. Model no:127)

Congratulations! You have just acquired
a looking-glass that will at once transform
your dressing-table into endless space
on which you will be frequently required
to replicate the contours of your face.

Amongst the things this mirror loves to see
are pretty, hand-worked mats in antique lace,
but dirty ashtrays, tepid mugs of tea,
false eyelashes, will cause the glass to bend
and fold up every corner of the room
shaping a place you do not recognize.

Treat your *'Desirée'* mirror as a friend.

Slide gold rings and/or gemstones every night
into a china bowl of perfect white.
And if the mirror-image should display
the most infinitesimal vibrations,
this is a consequence of exhalations,
mainly from emeralds. Turn out the light.

Treat your *'Desirée'* mirror as a friend
and keep it clear of every painful sight,
viz: balls of cotton wool, streaked with the traces
of substances removed from former faces;
all bloodstained walls; your mouth when you are lying;
anything broken; flowers close to dying.

Our guarantee does not, of course, extend
to objects that this mirror may reflect,
lengthen, enhance, distort, obscure, distend.

Ensure the face you offer to the glass
is fit for duplication. To this end,
treat your *'Desirée'* mirror as a friend.

The Dark and the Light

"One of the troubles with the world is that the inscription THEATRE is found in so few places."

Miroslav Holub.

We will believe in everything
hidden and unmoving in the dark:
cardboard trees, tissue-paper roses,
all the white palaces of fairyland
unrolling on the backdrop.
The corrugated velvet of the curtains
has soaked up hours of light,
faded into pink and crimson stripes.

We wait
for the magic seesaw of the dimmer-switch.
Where we are, dusk falls.
On stage,
rows of illusory small suns
rise in electric apricot and gold.

Photograph 1900

Poor M'sieur Robert! He's struggled with his camera
all afternoon: a concertina snout, black legs,
and more attendant paraphernalia than an infant.
He's putting it down for a moment, and no wonder.
Amelie (I can tell she's interested) shouts:
"Can we help you with that?"
"No, no, stay as you are. I want you
all four walking as if towards distant hills."
What does he see? Four dresses.
They will come out like this: one black, three white,
but Margot's is sweetly pink, Jeanne's mauve
and Amelie's is blue. If it were not for me,
we would be a family of sugared almonds.

The sun weighs on the silk slopes of my parasol.
Dust stirs around my feet; long, dry grass
pricks my skin, even through stockings.
"Don't move!" M'sieur Robert is excited.
Amelie vibrates. Oh, I can imagine sweat
in pearls all down her back, and how her flesh
when she removes her corset, will relax
to fancies of that hard, glass eye
sliding up her secret legs under waterfalls of skirt.

Papa and Maurice have walked on.
"There," says M'sieur Robert, lifting his metal baby
tenderly on to his shoulder. "I have it now."
The four of us, walking home.

We will have no faces, and perhaps
that's the truth of it. If we turned round now,
poor M'sieur Robert would die of fright.

Five postcards: La Guerre 1914-17 L.C.H.Paris

L.C.H. Paris photographed the War,
sent men to tiptoe over stones cracked open
(but oh, the mud on patent leather shoes
accustomed to sliding
round and round the ladies! The hands
that draped silk gowns alongside cardboard urns
and tucked undying flowers into décolletages
will touch raw air outside the studio.)

Pervyse, Nieucapelle, Reninghe, La Panne,
les ruines ... les ruines ... après le bombardement..

With difficulty on uneven ground
they found flat places,
covered their heads with black,
looked for something representative.

Here, a numbered bomb
blew the spy's house
to dust under a dune of bricks.
Only one corner, one last window
as they were.

Then
three grey church views:
free-standing arches rise in fields
of carvings scattered into shards.
Towers show white skies
through torn lace of masonry,
windows with no glass.

The brewery roof has gone, leaving
a lattice of timbers.

There's a soldier in this picture
embarrassed by his own survival.
Behind the camera, under the dark cloth
he imagines the head, a skull's curve.
He's propped his bayonet
against the sandbagged wall,
and made his own, much smaller conflagration:
lighting a cigarette,
breathing out the smoke.

Door

The gates are closed.
Behind black railings, marguerites
and lilies taper to dark stems.

Trees in stone urns
unfold new branches
on the white steps.

She has been offered
a side view of the house
and cannot see the door.

Beyond pale flowers
lost in long-shadowed leaves,
how the door might look

pulls at the edges of her thoughts
like something she's caught sight of,
disappearing. Gone.

Carpet

The waves end here,
sucking at silk fringes,
pulling away from the carpet,
from the straight shoreline
into darkness, into foam and green.
They will fill the shell curves,
wash the bone-garlands,
withdraw.

In this carpet there are:
one thousand hand-tied knots to the square inch,
maroon and gold and brown and peacock blue
triangles, cunningly placed. And
threading between the colour-blocks,
a tree of black lines
and white birds in black lines of branches —
seven white birds with tilted squares for wings,
set among rectangular leaves
and pentagons of fruit.

Isn't the world enormous in the lamplight?
Lie on the sofa
in cream light
and watch beyond the interlocking
inch-high mountain ranges
(maroon and gold and brown and peacock blue)
seven white birds unflying
over the water.

Just where the carpet ends
the waves begin.

Camellia

The first flower to open seems designed:
stamped out in wax and tinted with a brush
the pink of blushes, seashells and clichés.
From the dark heart towards the outer rim
small petals skim and lap and overlap,
a mesh of tiny, uncompleted rings
each broken by the curving of the next.

It's strayed into the garden by mistake,
fallen beyond the frame encompassing
a Chinese painter's dream of smooth and round.
This is a flower to tuck into your belt,
or wind into your hair with satin bands
before the fire of growing in the world
has scorched the edges of the petals brown.

The orange tree

This yellow afternoon
the maid has set a table
in the conservatory.
Tea cups float silver circles
on cream linen. Wisteria
falls away from mauve
to thinning twilight.

Someone placed a pip
in a jardinière
haunted by dragons.
Now surprising leaves
touch the glass roof
above the table.

Deliberately,
this yellow afternoon,
she wears a dress
matching the fruit

and waits
under her private chandelier:
quietly, in the light of oranges.

Going to Shaw on the train

Mona and Nile, Raven and Lilac, Briar and Dawn:
working or not, the cotton mills are named
like ships: tall letters calling over distances.

Metal echoes from the old machines
follow us down the rails.
Blue air with a white cloud print
unwinds behind brick chimneys as we pass.

In Shaw, someone points out the house for me.
The sisters who were murdered there
would have remembered them:

Mona and Nile
Raven and Lilac
Briar and Dawn

in the days of their glory.

Picture on a beermat from the Low Countries: oude gevels, anciennes façades

She took it home.
A filigree of ink cross-hatches bricks,
outlines diamond window-panes in black,
points roof-triangles towards white skies;
slopes down lines of steps to the canal.

She keeps it,
imagines mirrors multiplying tiles,
doubling the chessboard floor. A woman stands
in careful arrangements of furniture ,
her face, her hands turned to a source of light.

She looks at it.
Pulling the iron's sharp and silver heat
across the lapis lazuli of jeans,
she thinks of Dutch interiors, where lamps
stipple with gold the contours of the dark.

A cream tea in Devon

Raise your eyes
from the bone-china teacup,
from the small dishes where cream
lies lustrous on painted flowers.

Photographs of broken ships
cover the walls.
The camera stills slabs of moving sea,
and dwarfed by water fixed in grey cliffs and crags
figures in black stand ready for the worst.

There's the 'Queen Margaret', slanting
her three masts into
a corner of the frame:
drowning.
The Lizard. Maenheere Rock.
Nineteen-thirteen and the thirteenth of May.

Listen. Through the mists rising
from Darjeeling in a teapot on the table,
something howls.

Remains

Mother of pearl splinters
embed haphazard mosaics
in the lid of this small box.

My father used to put pipe cleaners in it
and little pencils with long memories.

I've kept a salt cellar also. The lid's gone,
but here's a galleon with blue sails set
riding the turquoise scrolls of painted waves
with two pale fishes silver in her wake.

Bridal

I walk in his garden
thinking of mountains.
Against the wall, trees grow
like open fans. Apricots
swell into the brick;
also dark hearts of plums
sweet with blood.

My hair is thin black snakes twisting
between the teeth of ivory combs.

At night, he unfastens my silver robe
swarming with silk dragons.
They have embroidered
with their claws of pearl
long scarlet seams of scratches
down my back,
over my breasts.

"A secret and ancient 'women only' script ... has been discovered in China where it is still in use. The script, using an inverted system of grammar and syntax, ... is written ... without punctuation. Locals claim the script was developed by Hu Xiuying, a concubine of the emperor Qinzhong ... she created the language to relieve her loneliness in the Imperial Palace."

(From a report in The Guardian by Jasper Becker)

A message from Hu Xiuying

apricot unexpected
on wall fan
trees spread never
in only dreams
see but smell now
walking silk dressing
in down his not gardens
mine faces wishing
on to walls into
birds pictures feeling
in not hair
pins wind waist
free water like
sash music falling
drums here pipes
singers longing
distance voices
home of shouting
mountains over
come

Xi'an 210 B.C. A sculptor at the court of the First Emperor speaks

Qin Shi Huang means to be remembered
and I am his unworthy instrument,
one of several sculptors
engaged on this ambitious project.
Each individual in the Imperial Guard
— archers and pikemen
sentries and officers
charioteers and even their horses —
is to be fashioned from the yellow clay
of the Yellow River.
Copied from life.

When he is buried
(the Emperor told me this himself)
his army will protect him.
Qin Shi Huang's ghost will look into each face
and recognize old friends.

Here is the first general,
life size.
He wears a long robe
and a cap shaped like a bird.
I have picked out
every scale on his armoured suit.
His shoes are square across the toes.
His hand is on his sword,
appropriately.

Recently, my mother has dreamed
of floods. She has seen the Yellow River
unfurling mud over the landscape.

She says she's seen my hand-carved soldiers drowned.
I tell her: these blind eyes
I've pricked into the clay
will watch time pass for ever.
These men will stand,
their shoulders stiff under the years.

The ceramics room

Eau-de-nil aquarium light
overflows each case,
watering down the dark.

Patterns slip and shine on the white swell of jugs,
travel over moon-wide plates; dip
silent as fish into the curves of bowls
glazed deeper than oceans.

These few remain
in quiet cubes of glass.
Salvaged: lifted clear
of the long wash of days.

Sampler

This is the sequence:
border, numbers, letters, name and date,
a thin, black motto for encouragement.

Learn simple stitches first (a slanting line, a cross,
arrangements of silk hyphens in long rows)
then fill the petals of rectangular flowers
sown on the pale grid of the cloth.

Make sure the back is neat, the stray ends cut.
There will be other places
for green, unravelling strands and knots of blood.

Egyptian cat

Observe the window edged and veiled with lace.
Your cat, who lies in curves to fit the bay
watches the minutes spiral through the day,
the people moving through a thin, grey space,
and in the houses opposite, pale lights like yellow eyes.

I am her ancestor. My eyes are blind
and in this pose I was designed to stand
thousands of years ago. A sculptor's hand
pushed me towards the cat-shape in his mind.
Like waves outside my small glass tomb, the sands of desert
rise.

Highgate Cemetery cat

I claw the silence open
with a small cry of recollected grief.

Ivy is a carpet,
marble a bed,
the hollows of a vault my cold shelter.

Moths flutter in my mouth,
blur on my tongue.
Old moons turn yellow in my eyes.

My lingering tail caresses
the thin names disappearing from the stones.

At dusk, I pace my territory:
through the grey shadows, over the white bones.

Voices from the dolls' house

Mama

Under a bell of figured brocade
is the hidden stiffness of my legs
but in an upper room
in the shade of brass branches
espaliered on the wall
my legs bend, give at the joints
and his woodenness is on me
over me under me and how locked
we are into silence and heat.
This room has wallpaper patterned
with birds. Their beaks are black.
The trees they sit in
have leaves as long and sharp as knives
and black like knives. Pomegranates
halfway from red to yellow
shine like small lamps,
but they have bitter seeds
set like teeth in pink translucent flesh.

My Baby lies in the nursery
next to the attic reserved for mad aunties.
She has a hollow head
but I say nothing.
Hollow isn't empty
and at night the space behind her eyes
thickens with little fluttering fears
that beat like moths: grey wings
against her eyelids.

I wish I could pack some brown valises
and go to Scarborough.
I would carry Baby

wrapped in waterfalls of lace
and we would all take tea in the Refreshment Room,
and everyone would say: 'Look!
Look at the Dunkerleys! How grand they are!'

I am dreaming of cliffs,
and the symmetry of walks
in summer parks.

Papa

I shall engage a photographer chappie
to compose a suitable image of the family.

I would like Alps in the background.
There's a lot to be said for mountains.

I shall wear a stiff collar up to my chin
and a gold chain across my waistcoat

of mulberry silk. I shall wax my moustaches
and put pomade on every single hair.

I'm proud of my son in his sailor suit
and of my daughter in a pink sash

from which there's no escape. The Baby
is pretty enough, what I can see of it,

and Mrs. Dunkerley is a woman to admire
especially (ho!) at night, when her legs

creak open, split, and she rises
against my body with short cries

like agonies of small white birds.
Thank God for that young Ida in the kitchen!

In the long intervals between basting the turkey
and kneading the dough, she's ready

always ready to lift her skirts, that one,
show her padded legs, her rounded bum

stuffed with soft cotton, always ready
for flopping, for soft and pliant moans

with the light of the flames from the oven
shining red on her whiteness.

If we could go on holiday, I would lean
(in the hotel) against the mantelpiece

every inch a gent. Both hands behind my back
my head held high. A twinkle in my eye.

Miss Edwina

Nothing escapes me.
I know what they're up to,
all of them. They put me
in frills and hope for the best
but I know.

Mama is nervous.
Papa is full of himself.
Mama does not know
what Papa does
with Ida in the kitchen.

Ida shakes when Papa
does it, like pink and white blancmange.
Her face goes red.

Up in the attic
(everyone has forgotten but me)
the aunts lie chattering
under what's left of their hair
about gravestones and
paste jewellery and rats
who live behind clouded mirrors
there. They have no visitors.

The aunts wear dresses
that are brittle with neglect.
The edges of their cuffs
are soiled, torn, have come away
from the sleeves. And
(I know they can do this)

they send dreams into Baby's empty head
and the dreams disintegrate
like moth wings in the dark. Baby's head
is packed full of dark.

Mama would like me to marry.
She thinks if we could go to Scarborough
someone suitable would appear.

I should like to go.
There would be waterlilies in the Refreshment Room
and I could dream of rivers
cool as glass, and the train
would blow bruise-coloured clouds into the sky.

Teddy

If we really could go to Scarborough
Papa would take out his watch
and show me what twenty minutes looks like.

It would look like a fat slice out of a pie
and that's how long we'd have
for tea before the train.

I want to see the sea,
chilly and grey and wrinkled.
I want to eat an ice-cream.

I would wear my sailor suit
and take my soldiers in the valise
safe in their painted box.

Then all the people on donkeys'ld stop
and say: 'Golly! what a tremendous battle!'
If any soldier died, I'd bury him

in the sand, and then unbury him again
when it's time to go home.
All I do now is look out of the window.

Baby

Under my eyelids:
a jack-in-the-box and
a humming-top and
marbles and
violet cachous and
a kaleidoscope where
Mama and Papa and Edwina and Teddy

and Ida the cook and the mad attic aunties
have been chopped into glittery, glittery pieces
and made to dance in glittery patterns.

I keep my eyes closed
because if I open them
the white birds on the wallpaper
will know exactly
where to put their beaks.

Ida

Soften the butter
add the sugar
cream them together
mix in the eggs and
ooh, he doesn't half fancy himself!
With his : 'Come now, Ida.'
(I know what that means!)
So I ups the petticoats
thank you kindly
and laugh while he riddles me
pokes me, puffs at me
for all the world as if I'm a fire
about to go out, and he's an iron.
Well, I like this house
so I do some grunting
some flopping and heaving
and all the time
I'm wondering whether the gooseberry fool
will stretch to six
for tomorrow's lunch.

The Aunties

Do you remember the dances, the candles,
the beaux and the carriages, fans and scarves?

We forget nothing, that's our trouble,
and every day there's more to remember
so that things to remember lie around us
like cobwebs in drifts and we hear the voices
and what they say.

The sounds break over us like blue waves
over ancient rocks and like blue waves the voices
leave a foam behind that froths like lace at first,
hardening later into memories.